P

Psychology

*Learning positive thinking in everyday life &
control your mind*

Understanding & overcoming fears

Analyze people & recognize manipulation

Psychology book for beginners

General Psychology books

Volume 1

Table of contents

Introduction

Why do people have such different characters, ways of thinking and behavior? One kind is on the sunny side of life. Everything they tackle, they succeed right away. It seems that they do not have to make a special effort to be successful in all areas of life.

The other kind has drawn the "loser" card in the game of life. Everything they try ends in unmanageable disaster. These people are treading water and have the feeling that the next disaster is already waiting for them around every corner. They have great fears and blockages that prevent them from getting ahead and ensure that their self-confidence and appreciation of themselves is only of a low intensity. Babies who have just seen the light of day may be equipped with different genes that they have inherited from their parents. But no infant is born as a sneak or a strong personality. These two things arise in development and are very much influenced by the environment in which the little people grow up. First, it is the parents who choose a style of upbringing to impart values and norms to the child.

Another factor is the environment, the school, the social class and the way of thinking of the fellow human beings, which influence the development of behavior and thinking patterns. Religious norms and values should not be underestimated.

Depending on their religious affiliation, women and men have a different status in the hierarchy. Politics and social influences also determine whether a person develops into a free thinker or clings to conventions without questioning them and seeking new ways to provide true happiness and satisfaction with oneself and one's life. Old, transmitted conventions and standards limit development because they manipulate people and show them again and again that there is only the one ultimate way to move forward. However, the fact that this path can be quite wrong is not considered.

In an earlier time, these things may have been good and right. But today they are no longer valid because not only the social distribution of roles has changed. Lifestyles have also changed. There is no longer just black or white, but many other colors.

These are not just the familiar shades of gray, but also bright, vibrant colors that simply make people happy and satisfied. They have found bliss in one or more decisions and hold on to it because they know that this is the right path for them. Make your world a little more colorful by recognizing yourself and your importance. Release blockades, say goodbye to your fears, open your eyes to recognize manipulation, try to understand people, analyze ways of thinking and behavior and find the right path for yourself into a happy, content life. If you want to do this, there are no more excuses. Because with positive psychology, you manage to find the obstacles that limit you.

Every person is individual, and everyone must decide for themselves where their ship will go but with the right knowledge of different influences, you can weigh up whether you dare to tread new paths and think outside the box.

Recognizing and releasing blockages

Mental blockages are insidious little beasts that hide in the subconscious. Although you notice that something is there that is slowing you down, you cannot recognize where this feeling comes from and why it is there. There is no way to make these insidious things visible, neither with an ultrasound nor with a TC or an X-ray machine. This is why it is so difficult for medicine and science to make mental blockages visible and thus tangible.

To handle and solve something intangible is a big task. The small ghosts make life unnecessarily difficult, cost a lot of strength and energy and cause stress. These factors hinder you in strengthening your self-confidence, gaining self-confidence, shaping your own life and making your person the priority. But there is a way to find and dissolve blockages.

This does not work like physical pain, where there are special drugs and painkillers. In order not to feel mental pain, people are real regressionists.

They paint even the worst fears with bright colors so that they don't have to look them in the malicious, sparkling eyes. But this is where the problems begin, which develop into a big monster, a mental blockade. But what are mental blockages? These are programs that run in your subconscious and hinder you in your thinking and acting. They arise in exceptional psychological situations that do not fit into the previous process. They cannot be processed so easily because there is too much mental pain. The subconsciousness creates behavior patterns to suppress this pain and to cope with it. You should defend yourself against this by confronting this emotional pain. Grab the burdensome subject by the hair and try with all your strength to let go and dissolve the blockages.

Because these malicious specters have a firm grip on you and prevent you from living a happy, fulfilled life.

Mental blockades

- you sabotage every step of the way.
- can be the cause of various diseases.
- cause certain problems to recur time and time again, giving you the feeling of being stuck in the same place.
- can be dissolved by a positive attitude.

Perhaps painful experiences in your childhood have led you to have mental blockages which as a teenager presented themselves as complexes, depression, low self-esteem and self-confidence. To release emotional blockages, you have to deal with the topic "letting go".

Set everything to restart with release

There are a variety of methods that you can use to learn to let go to release mental blockages. They work very well and will bring you a lot further. If it weren't for this one massive chunk that weighs you down. You cannot find a suitable lever to release this blockage and to strengthen your self-confidence. Just the right lever is the realization that you have to let go to dissolve the mental blockage completely and not to carry any more ballast around with you. But what is meant by letting go?

"Letting go means nothing more than saying goodbye to certain negative thinking and replacing it with positive thinking!"

You release yourself from a stressful situation, a negative event that causes you stress.

How does it work?

A small example:

You are on the full train on your way to work and have not been given a seat. You are in the corridor with many other people who are also on their way to work.

Suddenly the train driver has to make an emergency stop. The person standing behind you loses balance and pushes you rather roughly in the back, so that you have trouble stopping yourself. You are filled with great anger and rage. Why can't this person hold on properly to prevent such a situation? This bad feeling creates stress. You turn around to give the person a proper opinion and suddenly the situation has changed completely. Because before you stand a person with dark sunglasses and a cane for the blind. He is wearing a yellow armband with three black dots on his arm. Immediately your emotions change. The resentment and anger are neutralized and replaced by understanding and compassion.

What causes this change in feeling?
You have gained a different view of things because you previously misjudged the situation and assumed wantonness.

The new situation has allowed you to let go of anger, resentment and stress and replace them with new feelings without being aware of them. Your perspective has changed. To release mental blockages, you have to change your view of the situation or the event causing it. This neutralizes the stress hormone and the blocking feelings. More positive emotions arise.

However, it is not always easy to change one's perspective and manifest new ways of thinking because the injuries have too deep roots. It is important that you recognize why you react so negatively to certain situations. Maybe the blockage has nothing to do with external influences but is based on the fact that you are in your way and cannot jump over your shadow.

First try to find out the origin of the mental blockage. To do this, it is very important to find out the specific characteristics of the mental block.

Can you identify with the following points?

- When you are addressed by someone, the blush rises to your face.
- If you have to speak in front of other people, you are at a loss for words.

- During an exam you suddenly black out, even though you know the exam material inside out.
- Do you have the feeling of losing control when things don't go the way you want them too?
- Do tormenting memories and thoughts from the subconscious repeatedly emerge, which are connected with the past?

If you know one or more situations only too well, you are very likely to be emotionally blocked. It is precisely these that need to be resolved. Unfortunately, there is no magic potion that removes the inner blockades as if by magic. You have to become active and face these feelings. Do not try to ignore your emotions. By deciding, you set the course for the start of a life full of satisfaction and happiness. The first step is to roll up your sleeves and do something about the blockages.

You will succeed if you are convinced that you deserve a better life and do everything you can to achieve this goal. But just the decision is not enough. You have to do something about it.

Meet the challenges

The path to a new, better life begins with a powerful, energetic decision. This is that you dislike pain and do everything possible to counteract it. On this great path you will encounter small and also immense challenges, pitfalls, headwinds and many other adversities. It is important that you face and deal with them. Some insights you gain in the process are very painful. But the pain will be less and finally dissolving into pleasure because you can deal with the new knowledge in a completely different way. The small instructions will help you.

Important Info: *The manual is interesting for those people who have problems with other people and are looking for solutions. It cannot be used if traumatic experiences, such as abuse of any kind, have occurred. In the case of such experiences a therapist, doctor or alternative practitioner should be consulted to remove the blockage with their support.*

The Naikan method for the here and now

To gain self-knowledge, the Naikan method is a wonderful approach to positive psychology. Translated from Japanese, *"nai"* means inside and *"kan" means to* observe. Accordingly, Naikan is nothing else than the immersion in one's being. You explore yourself, learn to look inside, recognize and dissolve blockages.

There are four key questions that you can use to explore relationships with caregivers or specific issues. The special feature of the questions is that you do not look inwards from the perspective of the victim or perpetrator. You take a neutral position. This gives you a changed, neutral perspective on the elements that you are blocking. With the following four questions you can succeed in changing your life.

They are ideal if you have problems in partnership, at work, in sexuality, with money and other things. You do not have to turn your whole life upside down for this. Past things belong to the past and only exist in the brain. That is why you start in the here and now.

Life will take care of you and wrap blockages in educational gifts. Feel free to tear open the pretty wrapping paper and see what gift life is giving you right now, even if it can sometimes end painfully. The past is on the schedule later. If you ever get bored, you can approach the process of breaking up the relationship with your parents. So, save that for later. First of all, it's about the "now", which should have priority. The present is where the active life takes place. Find a retreat where you can think undisturbed. Look inside yourself and look, for example, at a person, a situation or events that cause you problems and stress. This emotional stress creates negative feelings. Take your pad and pencil with you to your island of rest and recall what this critical situation looked like. It is important that you look at the situation or event neutrally and do not immediately fall back into negative feelings.

Light up the situation or event with the following questions:

- What problems and difficulties have I caused this person?
- What have I done for this person?

- What has this person done for me during this time?
- What did I learn from the situation? (Could I grow through the event?)

Write down everything that comes to your mind about the person or situation. Chose sentences such as:

- the person (he/she) was disrespectful towards me
- I felt bad because...
- ...the person has given rise...
- I am not to blame...

Then you'll be a victim quickly. Strike those phrases from your vocabulary. You're the one who wants to make a new, different point of view.

But you can only do this if you look at the other side of the coin. Which problems have arisen for me through this person, fall quickly under the table because they seem irrelevant in the victim role? How this question system works can be illustrated most easily with an example.

Example:

You want to play football with your offspring in the garden and the adjacent garage of the neighbor, which borders directly on your meadow, is perfectly suited as a goal wall to shoot the balls against. Your neighbor dislikes this and starts to call you names. You immediately go into opposition, get angry and have the right answer at hand. Your neighbor is so angry that he threatens to call the police. Exactly At this moment you realize that the neighbor's aggression has also triggered aggression in you.

If you think about this situation in more detail and look at the questions again, you will quickly find out why the situation could have escalated in this way.

What problem did you cause the neighbor?

Shooting balls against the neighbor's garage wall annoyed him. He was working concentrated in the garage workshop and was constantly disturbed by the goal kicks. This disturbance creates stress, which is expressed in anger.

What did you do for your neighbor?

They took him seriously, listened to him, paid attention to him and his concerns and provided valuable time.

What did your neighbor do for you during this time?

He certainly had to summon up a lot of energy and courage to address you. And he has sacrificed as much time as you have.

What did you learn from the situation and how could you grow from this event?

One thing is clear! Your neighbor has created a situation through his anger in which you gain a deep insight into yourself. You quickly realize that you have aggression slumbering inside you that you do not want. This insight changes your perspective. You can learn something from every situation and through every other person. No matter what the situation, there is always a positive side, even if you are deeply hurt and disappointed in another person.

Healing things from the past

They have broken down the current blockades. Nevertheless, there are still obstacles that stand in the way of a happy, content life. Now is the time to look at the past and to take a closer look at it.

Two variants are available for this purpose:

- **Variant 1:** You go back to your birth and examine your entire life so far.
- **Variant 2:** You pick up a stressful situation or event that spontaneously comes to mind.

With the **first option,** you will certainly not remember everything that has happened to you in your life so far. Because the memory between 0 and 6 years is hidden in many parts behind opaque veils. Only a certain part can be easily recalled. Do not embellish the facts and do not leave out any elements. Use only the respective memories that the brain provides you with at that moment. As a first step, look at the relationship you had with your mother. Were you breastfed as an infant, were you bathed by her and did she change your diapers for you? As an infant, you were a helpless creature dependent on the mother's care.

Your mother provided much more than necessities. For nights on end she sat at your bedside or carried you around the house because you were crying or sick. She did many things to help you develop and become the person you are today.

When examining your life so far, you should concentrate on the positive things and circumstances. You make sure that the negative things get smaller and smaller. Try to concentrate on the positive things for at least 21 days. During this time you will gain a lot of knowledge about your caregiver, can let go and feel freer. Mistakes that the caregiver has made become easier to forgive. The resulting blockages gradually dissolve until they have disappeared completely. Get a notebook in which you can write down everything in a quiet hour. Write down certain age periods so that your notes remain manageable.

This allows you to set the period from
- 0 to 6 years
- 7 to 12
- 13 to 18
- Select 19 to 24 years.

During the first week, write down everything that comes to your mind about the four questions regarding your mother. In the second week you focus on your father and start the cycle all over again.

The **second variant** is used for stressful situations in the present and is applied to events that happened a little while ago. Even if it is a big challenge, you should try to remember the facts. If you can't remember the facts exactly, try to talk to the person who created the stressful situation. Through such a conversation many misunderstandings can be resolved and negative feelings eliminated.

Do not be disappointed if the other person refuses your request for a conversation. This is perfectly fine and should not inconvenience you. Always remember that not everyone is willing to cooperate. Perhaps the "no" will give you the impetus to ask the four questions again to gain a new perspective on things. Integrate the questions as an integral part of your everyday life. You will be amazed because you will activate the self-healing powers of the soul.

Learning to think positively

Positive thinking means nothing other than seeing the positive aspects of every situation and not letting negative thoughts arise in the first place. Positive thinking goes together with self-confidence. Confidence in yourself allows you to believe in your successes, the possibilities and gives you the strength to touch things that others consider unfeasible. Just look at all the great successes in history. Behind all of them is always positive thinking! There was one person who believed in a special possibility and implemented it. Positive thinking provides you with many advantages:

- You focus on good things that make you happy.
- Bad things, failures and dangers make you stop moving forward. Positive things, on the other hand, give new impetus to get up and move on. You remain capable of acting.
- Positive thinking keeps body and mind healthy.
- It boosts your self-healing powers so that you can defeat even the worst illnesses.
- Positive thinking and the optimism that goes with it are the best prerequisites for success in the professional and personal area.

- Positive thinking holds a nice lesson for you. You have the reins in your hands and can influence your thoughts to a certain extent. This means that you have completely new and undreamt-of opportunities at your disposal.

- A positive view of yourself and your successes strengthens your self-esteem and self-confidence.

- You are open for new things and thus broaden your horizon.

- Your sensory organs and your perception function much better through a positive way of thinking. With this you are ready to break new ground and not to close your eyes to it.

Many people roll their eyes when the topic of "positive thinking" is addressed. The reason for this is a completely wrong assumption about what positive thinking means at all. They believe that when you think positively, negative things are simply blanked out. This is wrong! It is just as wrong that positive thinking people are dreamers. Optimism is as real as pessimism. There is nothing in this world that is only positive. But it is important to know that even negative things have a positive side. You decide for yourself on which side you want to concentrate.

12 ways to finally think positively

1.) *Do not pay attention to negative thoughts anymore!*

As you already know, negative thoughts have great power and are destructive. They influence your mood, joy and courage and make you feel bad. Negative thoughts are not worth paying much attention to. This way you will not get lost, but you will receive a completely different weighting. If you once again conclude that self-reproach, fears and worries are spreading or that only negative thoughts are in the foreground, pull the ripcord very energetically and deal with other, positive things that distract you from the negative thoughts.

2.) *Smile!*

Again and again you meet people who go through life with hanging mouth corners and grouchy and again others who meet life with a grin on their face.

The people with a smile on their lips are the happier ones. Researchers have found out that a positive facial expression already releases happiness hormones. The brain absorbs the positive information transmitted by the facial muscles. Smiling makes you happier and more relaxed and you no longer see things just black, but in many other shades of color.

3.) Look for the good things in the situations that arise!

Every medal has two sides, just like every situation. That's why you can still get something good out of every bad experience, if you use the right interpretation. See negative things as a challenge and as a learning impulse. If you can't find a parking space right in front of your door, you can get excessively annoyed and grumble about it or enjoy a little walk in the fresh air after work. It may not always be easy to gain something positive from big, existential situations. If you have just suffered a great loss, the advice "it will be good for something" may not be very helpful.

However, if you have already looked more closely at small things and discovered the positive side, you will succeed even with bigger challenges.

4.) *Write a diary of the things you are grateful for!*

Not all things are always as bad as they seem at first. You are guaranteed to encounter many things for which you are grateful. You can write such things in your gratitude diary. This way you focus on the positive things instead of paying too much attention to the negative. Write down all the things you are thankful for in one quiet minute. It is not bad if you write down the same thing over and over again, the important thing is that you make yourself aware of it. With time, you will discover more and more positive things that you encounter in your life.

5.) *Use a considered dosage of negative information!*

No matter whether you turn on the TV and radio or browse social networks. Everywhere you look, you'll find disaster reports, so it's easy to get the impression that there's nothing positive in this world. Of course, there are violence and disasters, but there are also at least millions of positive things. They just don't show up on the news.

Just minimize the flood of negative news by not watching or listening to the news every hour and by only occasionally browsing social networking sites.

6.) Remove negative people from your environment!

Whether your attitude is positive or negative is closely related to the surrounding people. If you have people around you all the time, who are only bitching and moaning, you quickly adopt this attitude. It works the other way round as well. If you surround yourself with positive people, the positive attitude will rub off on you. So, look for the Sun Children and use positive psychology.

7.) Finally, climb out of the victim role!

Positively thinking people also take full responsibility for their lives and do not blame other people. Therefore, you should say goodbye to the thought that you are the victim and only the bad things happen to you. You have great influence on your life. That's why you should never let go of this important responsibility. You have the rudder in your hand and can determine where your ship is going.

Once you have gained the understanding with all its consequences, many chances and possibilities open up for you to take advantage of.

8.) *Avoid comparing yourself with others!*

Why does the neighbor have a nicer house and a bigger car and why is the colleague more successful than me? With these comparisons you create a nasty aftertaste that is guaranteed to make you sick to your stomach. You better take a good look around. Some people are much worse off than you. Unfortunately this is done far too rarely. People almost always compare themselves with people who are better off. Stop it! If you manage to do this, your basic attitude will automatically change and positive thinking will take over.

9.) *Use positive thinking for your success!*

Even if you are not even aware of it, you have already achieved so many things. Why not write down all your successes, even the smallest ones? These include your school-leaving certificates, the studies you completed with a master's degree, your driving license, bringing up your children, moving to a bigger, chic apartment and don't forget the difficult situations. There is guaranteed to be a lot of things involved. Add to the list again and again with new successes, whether it's the repaired faucet or the training session in the gym that is always put off. Write a daily list where you enter your successes. It is significantly more effective than a to-do list.

10.) Keep your needs and your limits in mind!

Positive thinking is difficult when others are constantly trying to exceed your set limits. Show your limits and needs clearly and always keep them in mind.

This important step ensures that you are good to yourself. This is the path of positive psychology.

11.) After getting up, concentrate on positive thoughts!

If you start the day with positive thoughts, everything will be much easier and nothing can throw you off tracks. For you to succeed, you should recall a situation early in the morning where you were well, where you were happy and satisfied.

Try to create the same feelings as you did then and enjoy this positive moment to the full.

12.) Read books that deal with the topic "Happiness" and "Being Happy"!

The topic of "positive thinking" and "being happy" covers much more than the points listed. Therefore, you should deal with the topic very intensively. With the appropriate literature you will have good helpers to help you rethink. Search for suitable literature in the bookshop or online. You will see that anyone who wants to can be happy.

Fears: far-reaching effects on a happy life

Fears are not only burdensome. They have a far-reaching effect on your development, restrict and prevent you from enjoying your life fully. They come in different forms. Experts agree that, depending on the degree of anxiety, the quality of life is so severely limited that people can perish from these negative feelings. Their subdivision of anxiety sometimes looks like this:

1. At the top of the list is **fear**, where the feeling is described as threat or danger. It is used to ward off harm and to avoid situations so that these feelings of fear do not occur in the first place.

2. A heightened form is **everyday fear**, which manifests itself in a threatening feeling that occurs at regular intervals when situations could get out of hand.

3. The **existential fear** is part of life and includes the fear of loneliness, death, curtailment of freedoms that take away your self-determination.

4. In the case of **neurotic anxiety,** for example, the fear of rejection arises.
    It is seen as a transition to a pathological form of fear. Sigmund Freud's definition of this fear is that man is afraid of a danger he has not yet experienced.

5. A **phobia is** a form of anxiety where concrete things and situations trigger the fear. This can be a confined space like an elevator, a spider, an exam or fear of social failure.

6. Obsessive thinking, behavior and action is called **obsessive-compulsive fear**. This includes, for example, the compulsion to wash, compulsive order or the compulsion to cleanliness.

7. Situations that cannot be psychologically processed or prevented cause **traumatic fears.**

   These include natural disasters, accidents, massive violence and sudden, serious illness. These anxiety states can come up again and again, even decades later. Experts call this "flashback".

8. **Generalized fears** accompany the affected person 24 hours a day. They wake up in the morning with these feelings and go to bed with them in the evening. There is no identifiable trigger for these anxiety states or a whole series of triggers, so that fear is permanently present.

9. **Panic attacks** suddenly appear out of the blue. On the one hand, there is a concrete reason for them and on the other hand, they can occur completely unprepared. They are based on a psychological and physical reaction and usually do not last longer than a few minutes.

10. Fears, coupled with a **personality disorder**, are based on the fear of losing the ego, the self and identity. This leads to a loss of stability.

These ten forms of fear are just some fears that accompany people through life. To be able to do something about these fears, you must first find out what they are based on.

Is this the **primal fear that** every person has? It is innate and prevents you from doing things that will only harm you. The primal fear is controlled by instinct. It is, for example, the fear of pain or death and ensures survival. Or is it fictitious fear that is only a pure imagination? Your fantasy shows you horrible pictures in different situations, which are spreading in your thoughts. They have no connection with reality and are exactly the opposite of the primal fear, which is quite justified. If your fears are fictional, there are many things you can do yourself to control them. Because the horror scenarios only happen in your head and do not have to occur in real life. Your thoughts create negative images and feelings of fear.

Imagine positive images of the event or situation and the fear will not take you over. There are different methods to combat fictional anxiety and make sure that the feelings of anxiety disappear.

7 methods to combat fear

For you to succeed in fighting your fears, the 7 methods start where fear arises, namely in your head.

1.) Do the reality check to counter your fear!

On closer inspection, most fears are completely exaggerated if you take a closer look at them during a reality check. You will quickly notice that in reality nothing bad is caused by it. You can do the Reality Check easily by asking yourself whether the situation is really dangerous and what the worst thing that can happen to you is. The following examples show that your fears are unfounded:

⇒ **fear of making a mistake:** *Making a mistake is human. Besides, it always depends on the point of view. If you have made a mistake, you can always correct it again.*

⇒ **Fear of change:** *Change does not mean danger, but rather opportunities to rise above oneself. Through change, you develop yourself further and broaden your horizon.*

⇒ **Fear of new things:** *You can only develop further if you try new things. Even if the fear feels very real, you don't know what to expect beforehand. If you seize the opportunity, you will find out afterwards that your fears were completely wrong. That's why you should try new things.*

⇒ **Fear of showing boundaries:** *Calmly show your counterpart limits he must not cross and don't be afraid of them. The other person will neither attack you nor hurt you and will quickly recognize that he or she has behaved improperly.*

⇒ **Fear of showing the true personality:** *Nothing bad will happen, guaranteed, if you show your true personality, your true self. Every person is individual and does not need to hide for this. People who do not like their true self do not belong in your environment.*

⇒ **Fear of approaching other people**: *The only thing that can happen to you is rejection. Being rejected is not a great feeling, but it shows you directly that these people have little respect. You do not need such people.*

Make it clear to yourself that although it is an unpleasant feeling, it will not cause you further harm.

⇒ **Fear of failure:** *Failure and failures are not something that will cause you physical harm. See defeats as a challenge to grow and become better. They open up new perspectives for you. So get up again and start from scratch.*

⇒ **Fear of being alone:** *Even though it feels terrible, you don't have to be afraid of being alone. Make yourself aware that being alone being a pleasure because you finally have time for yourself, to fulfill your desires and to reorder your life.*

⇒ **Fear what others think about you:** *This fear is not only unjustified, but completely senseless. You should not care. Besides, most people have enough to do with themselves and are guaranteed not to think about you.*

⇒ *Fear of public appearances, presentations and job interviews:*

The worst thing that can happen to you are booing, shaking your head or perhaps being pelted with rotten eggs. Try to be convincing and create positive images in your head. The fear is only based on fictitious fears that can be influenced.

These are just a few things that feel uncomfortable. You create these feelings yourself in your head, but they do not cause you to feel real pain or be in danger.

As soon as you ask yourself what could happen to you in the worst case, you will find that the images in your head do not correspond to reality at all. Once you re-alize this, the fears lose their powerful effect.

2.) Change the pictures in your head!

In addition to the reality check, you can positively change the images in your head. The belief that you do not influence your thoughts is wrong. If you want to, you can control your thoughts.

Imagine a colorful flower meadow. Bet that you can see it right now in front of your inner eye!

All you need is the awareness that you are responsible for your thoughts. As soon as fear sets in, you should consciously perceive the images in your head and look closely at what they show. If they spread fear, try to erase them. You can do this by making the picture small or indistinct, tearing it up or painting over it with bright colours. If you keep trying to do this, it will be easy for you. Try to replace the negative images with positive ones. You can do this by imagining the seemingly negative picture in the most beautiful colors. Through your imagination you create a positive perception in your thoughts and thus replace the negative thoughts. Mental images are the best secret weapon against fears.

3.) *Learn to control your thoughts!*

The more aware you are of your thoughts, the easier it is for you to influence them. A excellent method for more awareness of your thoughts is meditation. With meditation, you can get off the merry-go-round of your thoughts and simply let go of negative emotions. It provides peace and more attention. You do not need to meditate for hours for this. A few minutes a day is enough.

In addition to mental peace and relaxation, meditation also creates a positive feeling in the body, which also has a great effect on feelings of fear.

Info: *If you are loose and relaxed, you cannot feel fear simultaneously!*

4.) Use success against fear as a secret weapon!

Feelings of success are a good way to fight fears. Each time you have overcome fear, you will have fewer negative feelings the next time. You feel that nothing bad can happen and develop a new self-confidence. Do this step by step before you face the big fears. To succeed in fighting fear, you can recall experiences of success. Remember situations where you have faced and overcome your fear. These do not have to be big things. Even the small things have an immense effect. The certainty alone makes you feel good because you have fought the fear of a certain event yourself. By remembering such situations again and again, you manifest them in your subconscious:

"I can do this, no matter what happens!" With this you will achieve that there will be nothing more to be afraid of.

5.) *Face your fears together!*

Sometimes fears grow when you have to face them alone. For example, you may find it much worse when you have to talk alone in front of an audience or when you go home alone in the dark than when you are with other people. A group gives you a secure feeling and support. This makes you feel significantly stronger yourself. Find people in your environment who are not afraid of situations or things that scare you. In the same way, you can surround yourself with people who have already overcome fears. They show you that you can face your fears without something terrible happening.

6.) *Counteract your negative thoughts by acting!*

The more you think about a situation, event or thing, the more fear builds up. This is quite logical, as you spend a lot of energy on imagining negative images in your mind. Be quicker than your thoughts and get in the fast lane so as not to conjure up the worst scenarios any longer.

This does not mean that you are rushing into danger. Keep the time of thought to a minimum and ask yourself if the thing or situation is threatening. Then you should do it! Speak to the fascinating woman or the great man next to you at the bar, without having to go through 1,000 variations in your head.

There is no right or wrong. The only thing that can happen is that you get a rejection! Go on stage in a karaoke bar and grab the microphone before negative thoughts arise about how the audience might react. By acting immediately and being courageous, you will banish negative thoughts and horror scenarios from your mind.

7.) Let the pain of negative feelings take effect!

Of course fears are not nice feelings. But what alternative is there to counteract them. Fear has you firmly in its grip and prevents you from rising above yourself and breaking new ground. Try to face your fear and let the pain come. You can do this by imagining your life before your inner eye if you do not face your fear and fight it.

Try to feel the sensations that arise. Think about it,

- what you're missing out on because of your fears,
- what experiences you will miss
- and what restrictions on the quality of life the fears bring with them.

Those are not pretty performances!

Now imagine how happy and fulfilled your life will be when you have overcome your fears. Create images of how much more fun you will have in life when the fears are gone. Without fear, you can finally formulate new goals and realize them. In you is the potential to finally start a happy, contented life.

Learning to understand yourself and using this knowledge for personal development

There are these famous, simple statements that make you think and provoke dissatisfaction. One such statement is:

"Before I can change, I must first know myself!"

But what does it mean to know oneself? If you are honest now, you will soon realize that your way of thinking and acting can be very puzzling. You can confidently give up the claim to know yourself. But during your life you will always learn something about yourself and thus have the opportunity to change something. It is astonishing that people are capable of change, even if they think they don't know themselves at all and don't understand their actions. As confusing as this may sound, people can change because they reflect on their way of thinking and acting and find that they gain some awareness. There is clarity which deepens the own self-image. Self-knowledge arises, for example, through other people who give feedback on their person, behavior or expressions.

This does not mean criticism, but rather the concrete observations that other people make when dealing with you. However, your effect on other people is only one point among many others. It is also important whether the image of others and your image of yourself go together and whether you succeed in conveying your views correctly.

To develop self-image, you need to answer the following questions:

- Who am I?
- What kind of person am I?
- Why am I like this and not different?
- What can become of me?

One of the most difficult questions in terms of content and methodology is that of *"why"*.

This often reflects communication patterns that you have been confronted with in your life and still are. There are special patterns that are not very helpful for self-discovery.

These include questions such as "Why are you doing this again?" or *"How could you have...?* Such questions embarrass and distress you.

Let's go back to the original question. If you want to change something, you can change something even without a concrete goal. Something better can result from such an attempt. However, the efforts will be more effective if you understand the concrete connections. You can achieve this with a behavioral analysis. Many people think that this is very limited but on closer examination, it becomes clear that the questions about the "why" are not only superficial but go into depth. In doing so, you will gain a comprehensible explanation and information for some behavior, which will reinforce this behavior. Sometimes other people are the reinforcers who react to your behavior. That is why some people make a lot of nonsense just to get noticed and applauded.

Self-understanding also means that you get to the bottom of the question which mechanisms are responsible for your behavior. If it turns out that behavior patterns are only used to attract attention, you have a tangible means of changing your behavior.

If you see yourself as a person who orientates himself towards others and does things which do not correspond to your ideas, you must gain insight and accept this orientation. Ask yourself the questions whether what you do makes sense and whether you want to do it.

Understanding oneself, therefore, means nothing more than dealing with one's inclinations and views and creating clarity. With this clarity you get a view of things and can decide whether to change or maintain your life program. If you decide to be different, you come a lot closer to yourself and get to know yourself a little better again. That is why you should eliminate things you don't want from your life and only do the things you want! Ask yourself again and again whether you want to do that and what you truly love!

In this way you lay the foundation for developing a better understanding of yourself and expanding your personality. In addition to self-knowledge and knowing yourself better, you also need a certain degree of knowledge of human nature to gain a better understanding and appreciation of others.

Gaining knowledge of human nature and using it to achieve one's own goals

Knowledge of human nature is also an interesting topic in positive psychology. Because emotionally intelligent people see the world with completely different eyes. They can perceive, influence and understand the feelings of others. People with emotional intelligence are true leaders because they can control their emotions and the feelings of others to achieve goals.

In many cases, we believe that one look is enough to be able to assess another person. However, to recognize how the other person really ticks, a closer look is necessary. Because first impressions can be deceptive. The first glance is only a spontaneous assessment made from the present moment. This shows only a small section. You only look behind the façade when you have good knowledge of human nature.

Great temptation and lurking dangers

The great temptation is to look another person in the eye and be able to tell immediately what makes that person tick. It is tempting to be able to tell with just one look whether the other person is happy, sad or anxious and what makes up their personality. Unfortunately, this is not possible so simply. Reading faces is a lesson that has fascinated people since ancient times. Among the oldest records are writings by Aristotle, who dealt with this subject.

The assumption leads to the fact that mental characteristics are quickly deduced from a person's appearance in a fraction of a second. The quick shot leads to a misjudgment and rapidly stirs up prejudices. That is why real knowledge of human nature and not just half-knowledge is required! In the past, so-called physiognomy was considered an art and secret knowledge. It was mainly used by priests for occult purposes. In later eras, when the Enlightenment was at the forefront, this branch of expressive psychology became more important and was increasingly recognized as a scientific teaching.

Unfortunately, the new findings in physiognomy, which came to light through science, led to terrible consequences. They were not used to put oneself in other people's shoes better, to cultivate a more sensitive approach and to meet differences with appreciation. Rather, it was used in the 19th and 20th centuries to underpin racism and eugenics on a scientific level.

First indication of knowledge of human nature

The shape of the head, the width of the mouth or the height of the forehead are said to indicate characteristics such as willpower and intelligence. This assumption is still causing a lot of discussion in social psychology because experts believe that it does not lead to a better understanding of other people. Numerous studies also come to different conclusions.

However, there is one point on which the experts agree: The first judgment you make about another person is superficial. But it can be used to give a rough outline of the other person's personality. This first judgment you make about another person can be a protective mechanism derived from evolution. Before you let another person get closer to you, try to protect yourself. You look at him/her more closely and decide intuitively because of the first impression whether the person means well with you or is to be seen as an enemy. While this initial assessment is useful, it is only a first indication based on your feelings and assessment.

Reading emotions in the face of the other person

To better assess other people, the US psychologist Paul Ekman has developed a method called *Facial Action Coding System (FACS)*.

It dates back to 1978 and allows you to identify seven basic emotions from the muscle movements in your face. According to the psychologist, they are present in every person. These include fear, anger, surprise, disgust, sadness, joy and contempt. Today, many computer programs for emotion recognition are based on the FACS method. However, the method is rather controversial, as it does not consider that facial expressions can be controlled. That is why critics assume that there is no way to make a correct assessment with it.

Taking your influence into account

If you want to assess another person correctly, you must be aware that this does not work at first glance because you are not capable of looking at the other person neutrally.

Your evaluation is based on what you see and on yourself or your mood, your experiences and cultural background. People rashly put other people into a certain drawer, although they still lack a lot of information that justifies this sorting. Always remember that the outward appearance does not give a view of inner values. To recognize these, you must look more closely and ask questions. How does the person deal with other people? What are his ideals? What is important for him?

Proceed with care

Especially when it comes to things that seem important to you, you should exercise care and not make a hasty assessment or judgement. Even if you think you have good knowledge of human nature, you may be completely wrong with your assessment. You do not influence the first, spontaneous impression. However, you can use the first impression to take another closer look and possibly revise your first opinion. This is a fair trade. It can even be a great asset to you. At second glance, people who have judged you hastily may turn out to be wonderful, valuable people.

5 tips to improve your judgement

1. Remain open and alert, and always remember that you never look at others objectively. Your approach is based on your experience.

2. Appearances are no indication of a person's personality. Attractive does not mean that this person is also smart, fat does not mean that the person is funny. These are just clichés into which people like to quickly classify other people.

3. Question your prejudices. Because quite unconsciously you judge people or age groups without having reflected on them because your way of thinking is shaped by prejudices.

4. Train empathy. Before you give a negative evaluation about another person, you should try to put yourself in their place.
    Why does this person react like that? What is behind it? What is the reason for his action?

5. Also listen for overtones in the conversation. They reveal a lot about the other person. That's why you should listen carefully and recognize how the other person says something. This will tell you a lot about the character.

Manipulation: Covert influence on thinking and acting

Are you aware of the situation that you suddenly express opinions, utter utterances and certain ways of thinking appear, which sometimes do not correspond to your normal thinking and acting in any way and are contrary to your nature? Then you have met a person who is a master of manipulation. You encounter manipulative people everywhere and you do not even notice that thoughts and opinions are implanted in your head. You have become a puppet of your partner, friends, work colleagues or a speaker who influenced your way of thinking and acting with great persuasive power.

Manipulation is composed of the Latin terms "manus" (hand) and "plere" (fill) and has the meaning of "handling". The meaning in the sense of "handling" is still used today. In sociology, politics and psychology, manipulation is understood to mean the concealed exertion of influence.

Those who manipulate other people use a sophisticated approach, concealing the real motives, which are often self-interest, to gain an advantage and achieve a certain goal. Manipulative behavior does not necessarily have to be accompanied by a disruption. However, if it is extreme, it may be an antisocial personality disorder, such as narcissism. If other people are used as a tool to use manipulative, deceptive behavior for their benefit, the appearance of the disorder counts as a psychopathic disorder.

Influence is the often used synonym for manipulation. However, the factor of targeted exploitation is missing. Politics, for example, uses influencing to influence the population in their views and actions and to disseminate ideological ideas. Political influence is also known as propaganda. If you go back in recent history, you will find a frightening example in Nazi propaganda. Emotional influencing of other people for one's profit in no way corresponds to the basic idea that every person has for himself. Everyone wants to make decisions autonomously and freely, based on their passion and reason. They should not be the result of manipulation.

9 Signs of manipulation

Many factors can help you determine whether your counterpart is trying to manipulate you. The psychological manipulation manifests itself in the following behaviors, among others. You do not get an answer and your conversation partner resorts to sarcasm. You are told that it is impossible to talk to you or you are spoken to as if you were a child. Your interviewer gives you an ultimatum.

Especially in communication and language many kinds of psychological manipulation are hidden. By using them, people go on the path of emotional abuse and mental exploitation. Some people master the abuse of language perfectly and can control, guide and direct people. This was also demonstrated by the neo-fascist Licio Gelli in the history of Italy, who specialized in manipulating large masses of people. Accordingly, you only need to know how to communicate properly to gain control over other people.

Quote:

"Thoughts corrupt what is said, and what is said can corrupt human relationships."

George Orwell

Everyone knows such everyday situations only too well. Because you are exposed to constant manipulation in many areas, whether in politics, the media or through great advertising promises. A goal is thereby to influence you in your decision to seduce and control. Significantly more versatile and fuller of secrets is the manipulation, which takes place in the private sector.

In conversation with your partner, friends and other family members it has a perfect, mature camouflage, so that the trap snaps shut rapidly, or you use it yourself. It is therefore important that you look carefully at what you say and handle manipulative statements with care. Therefore, pay close attention to the choice of your sentences. In general, you should know how to detect psychological influence and react to it correctly.

Recognizable features of psychological influence

If verbal psychological manipulation occurs, there is an imbalance in the relationship between you and your interlocutor. The other person wants to gain a personal advantage through language, control you or even harm you. The resulting feelings generate hidden aggression not only in the other person, but also in yourself, which makes all signals to attack. Words have the great power to penetrate everything and do not even stop at the identity, self-esteem or dignity of the other person. To help you recognize psychological manipulation, you will now learn how to expose it.

1. **Facts get twisted!**

   Manipulative people who have perfect mastery of psychological influence are unique strategists and have perfect mastery of twisting the truth in their favor.

In doing so, they place the main blame on the shoulders of the interlocutor and reduce his share of responsibility. Important facts do not come to the table at all or are exaggerated. The adjustment is made to such a high degree that it corresponds exactly to one's perception of the truth.

2. Accusing that it is impossible to talk to you!

Behind this statement is not only directness but also effectiveness because the interlocutor refuses to talk about a problem. You are accused of being far too emotional and of making a big deal out of a little thing. With such statements you are blamed, even though the other person is the guilty party. This is evidence of a lack of communication skills.

3. Bullying at an intellectual level

Manipulators also like to use communication strategies that are on an intellectual level. You are continuously bombarded with all kinds of information, arguments, twisted logic and facts, which have only one goal: to emotionally exhaust you until you are convinced that your interlocutor is right.

4. **Set an ultimatum with a tight timeframe**

   Statements such as "You have until tomorrow to think about it" and "If you don't want to accept what has been said, this is the end of it" have probably already been said to you. Such comments are incriminating and hurtful. You will soon find yourself in a quandary that brings emotional suffering and fear. Always remember that a person who truly loves and respects you will never expect an all-or-nothing decision from you. People you try to manipulate in this way do not belong in your immediate environment because they only harm you.

5. **Repeat the name of the person opposite you constantly in conversation!**

   The constant, continuous and exaggerated repetition of your name in conversation is an indication of a clever control mechanism. This is intended to ensure that you listen attentively and are better able to intimidate.

6. Humiliation with black humor and irony!

Your interlocutor mocks you by injecting black humor and ironic remarks into the conversation. This kind of psychological manipulation serves to belittle you, undermine you and play on his superiority. In other words, the aggressor tells you that you are not equal to him and therefore you cannot have your opinion.

7. Feigning ignorance

A classic for feigned ignorance is the sentence: "I don't know what this is all about!" Your conversation partner pretends to be stupid and pretends to have no idea what it is all about and what you want to achieve with the conversation. Attention! This is where your mind is being played with. You are confronted with the accusation that you only complicate things and that a conversation is completely pointless. This strategy is often used by aggressors to make you suffer and not to take responsibility.

8. Your conversation partner gives you the right of way in the discussion!

Even if this psychological manipulation is subtle, the strategy has a particularly large impact. Because the interlocutor achieves two things with it. Firstly, he has gained enough time to react to your statements and arguments and meanwhile he can identify weak points to strike this notch. Sometimes, however, the manipulator also refrains from expressing his opinion and thoughts.

Questions are merely asked, and shortcomings are looked for, rather than finding a constructive common solution. By this way of manipulation the interlocutor succeeds in making you feel like a weak, clumsy person. Psychological and emotional manipulation has many more, unexpected facets.

But the listed ones belong to the common methods you will encounter again and again. They are used to intimidating and thus prevent a meaningful exchange in conversation.

The strategies put you out of action on a mental, personal and emotional level. It is therefore of immense importance that manipulative strategies are recognized and that they are resisted.

Ways of defense against covert manipulation

Dubious procurement of information

If your interlocutor tries to sound you out and the conversation resembles an interview, the communication aims at gathering information. At first, the impression may arise that this person wants to know more about you. This is often a good thing, if the ulterior motive is not to use the information to manipulate you. For manipulation to succeed, your weak points must be known. The manipulator will never reveal his weaknesses and will only show you his strengths. Be careful what you say. The aggressor will exploit your weaknesses. He doesn't care if it harms you.

Defense option: Avoid that the communication is only one-way and show the interlocutor that you have just as much right to know something about him or her.

A successful conversation is not a questioning game, but communication based on mutuality. Only tell as much about yourself as you want to reveal.

Resist the persuasions that corner you and tempt you to reveal more information. Ask the interviewer and counter his questions with counter-questions. This way the manipulator quickly realizes that he cannot intimidate you and you defuse the situation.

False truths

Manipulative people often tell stories that never happened and try to give you information that is simply wrong. Unfortunately, this is not recognized immediately. Manipulators do honor to the lie baron von Munchhausen and do not even have a bad conscience. To unmask such a person, you should take a close look at the purpose of the information and facts. A liar sometimes exposes himself because he answers unimportant questions excessively, justifies and explains. When situations arise that denounce the liar and question his or her honesty, he or she will have to justify himself or herself verbosely so that he or she is not put in the wrong light.

Defensive option: *If you think you have a manipulative character in front of you, you can expose it quickly. If a statement seems dubious to you, take the opportunity to ask questions. If the interviewer becomes nervous and evades your questions, you can almost assume that the story is not true.*

Targeted follow-up and questioning causes the manipulative character to get out of the line of fire.

Exaggerated charm

One of the greatest weapons of manipulation is charm. If you come across someone who pays you charming compliments, you can almost certainly assume that your conversation partner is a manipulator. Take a close look to see if there is something else behind the charm or if this person is naturally charming towards other people.

Selfishness hides behind charm when

- You receive compliments before a request is made,
- the person is only there for you in such situations if he/she enjoys advantages from them,

- would like the gesture to give him an advantage,
- the charm is only used in certain situations and
- little or no charm is used in other situations.

If these points apply to your interlocutor, he or she has only selfish motives, which he or she wants to enforce with charming behavior.

Defense: *Don't be blinded by the charming behavior of your conversation partner but observe his behavior and question why he is so charming right now. Charm should not be entangled with conditions or prerequisites. If the person you are talking to is charming, you do not need to see this as an obligation. You can say "no" if he comes around the corner with a favor or a request after a charming offensive. Prevent that your good nature is exploited and that the manipulator gets everything from you through his charm.*

A closer look at role patterns

People who want to take advantage of you often appear as martyrs. They present themselves as good-natured, self-sacrificing and helping people. Such persons appear sympathetic and receive all compassion. In this way they have opened all doors to manipulate you. The aggressor has quickly recognized where your weaknesses lie and uses them for emotional blackmail. He has recognized what he can use to hurt you and criticize you in a targeted manner. In this way he creates a feeling of inferiority in you, which often results in an emotional obligation. You do everything to please this person.

A flimsy basis of trust can also be a sign that your conversation partner wants to manipulate you. Another sign of manipulation is when the other party entrusts you with a secret and later expects something in return. Listen carefully to find out whether the secret entrusted to you is only used to obtain important information from you. He will use this information against you later. If you do not play the role intended for you, you will be immediately ignored and punished with contempt.

Defense: *If you feel that your interlocutor wants to push you into a certain role in which you feel compassion and simultaneously are asked for a favor, all the alarm bells should ring immediately, and these should please be rung out. A favor is given to another person for unselfish reasons, not because you have a guilty conscience. Take a position when you realize that you only want to be told secrets, stick to your opinion and do not trust blindly or hastily.*

Are you free in your decisions?

Manipulators can significantly influence your opinions and decisions.

To recognize whether you are being manipulated, you should take a closer look at your freedom of decision.

- Did the decision fall entirely on your initiative?
- Is your decision influenced by external influences and pressure from outside?
- Is your opinion formed by the influence of a particular person?
- Do you have the feeling that you might disappoint someone with your decision?
- Are consequences of be expected if you have a different opinion?

If the answer to the questions is "yes", you know that there is a manipulation of your freedom of decision and that your needs and feelings are no longer the main focus. Your feelings and needs are not relevant to the manipulator, since he is only pursuing his goals. They fall by the wayside and are only a means to an end.

Defensive option: *Prevent another person from making decisions over your head.*

If you think your decision is good and right, trust your judgment and do not let yourself be circumcised. You are endowed with common sense. Just because the other person believes he or she is right, does not necessarily mean that your opinion is wrong. Analyze your decision and consider why it turned out the way you did. Under no circumstances let yourself be changed if you stand behind your opinion with conviction.

Are you treated respectfully?

If you are treated respectfully, there is no pressure or coercion. Manipulative people tend to make threats to pave the way for themselves and influence others emotionally. Means such as promises of love or withdrawal of love are used to make you compliant. You are made to feel that you are responsible for how respectfully you are treated and how much affection you receive. The manipulator makes you feel that you have to expect consequences if you do not meet his expectations. He uses if-then sentences, expresses his disappointment through subtle punishments and takes a detached attitude towards you. There is no consideration for your feelings and needs, since only the needs of the manipulator are in the foreground.

Ward off: *Prevent you from becoming emotionally dependent in a relationship. It is important that people face each other on an equal footing and do not try to influence or bend the other person by threats or punishments. If you are disrespectful, let objectivity and prudence take precedence and remain true to yourself.*

Are comparisons made between you and other people?

Making comparisons is also a method that manipulators like to use to push you in a certain direction.

When you hear the sentence: "If you had done it the way XY said, things would have turned out very differently", this is an indication that the speaker wants to influence you. He is trying to present your path as questionable and to put you in a bad light. The confrontation is intended to create a feeling of inadequacy in you to bring about a change in behavior.

Ability to defend: *Show boundaries and declare that it is neither factual nor fair to make comparisons between you and another person. Feel free to tell the manipulator that he or she is hurting you by doing so and that it is disrespectful. Make it clear that you are an individual personality and therefore do not want to be lumped together with others.*

Feelings of guilt

Manipulation is the art of evoking feelings of emotional commitment and guilt in others. Therefore, you should pay close attention to your emotional world.

The following questions will help you to detect manipulation:

- Do situations arise again and again where you have the feeling that you have to apologize?
- Do you always have a guilty conscience only when your conversation partner tells you to?
- Does your conversation partner never admit to his mistakes?
- Are you being always blamed and made the scapegoat?
- Does a little misconduct turn into a big drama?

If you answer all these questions with "Yes", you will most likely be manipulated. Guilt and a guilty conscience create an emotional obligation that you want to use to rectify the situation. A manipulative person uses your mistakes and weaknesses to his advantage and makes you believe you are in his debt. Taking responsibility and admitting mistakes is very difficult for aggressors.

By assigning blame, a power imbalance is created so that the person who manipulates takes on the role of victim. This creates a huge amount of power. You are plagued by your guilty conscience and are therefore ready to pull out all the stops to make the alleged wrongdoing right again.

Defense: *Develop a special sensitivity for your emotions and insist that you are also allowed to be hurt and disappointed and want to communicate this openly. Prevent your interlocutor from accusing you of being the culprit and blaming you for everything. You have the opportunity to take over the conversation. With the right questions, you can reverse the role relationship.*

- *Do you think it's right that you always play the victim?*
- *Have you ever asked yourself the question, what kind of feelings does this cause in me?*
- *What purpose is there in you always making me look guilty?*
- *Do you think it's okay to always create this particular image of me?*

Manipulation only works as long as you give the other person the opportunity. Develop sensitivity for people in your environment and look closely at the motives. Is the action altruistic or is manipulation hidden behind it? If you feel that you are being manipulated, the best defense is attack. Speak your mind unambiguously and stand by yourself. No one has the right to use you for his benefit.

Positive psychology and the first tentative steps to finally enjoy emotional freedom

Every person carries his package with him, which he has not always tied himself. In some cases, it is the legacy of upbringing, social norms, religious affiliation and misguided attitudes that constitute seemingly insurmountable walls. These manifested basic ideas restrict you in your way of thinking and the development possibilities of your personality. You lack self-confidence and self-esteem. There are fears and blockages because you do not trust yourself. Investigate the causes and find out the reasons that limit you. Reflect on yourself and your immediate surroundings. There will always be new stumbling blocks. Every time you get up again, you will come a little closer to personal freedom.

Positive Psychology

Positive psychology, what is it? It is exactly the right lever to release blockages that restrict you in your development. It is just as effective in overcoming fears and finally breaking new ground.

With this positive psychology you will learn to understand yourself much more and gain an understanding of the way other people think and behave.

Manipulation, fear and blockages

It creates a very good basis for you to recognize manipulation by other people. Manipulation, fear and blockages are major obstacles that slow you down in your personality development and prevent you from gaining self-confidence, self-esteem and acceptance. With positive psychology, you get the best tools to finally break new ground and enjoy life. You free yourself from old burdens and look positively into the future. You look forward to the challenges that life offers you and gain a great deal of self-knowledge. You learn to appreciate yourself with all your mistakes and weaknesses.

Max Krone
Volume 1 (Positive Psychology)

Volume 2 (Manipulation & body language)
Volume 3 (Psychology for beginners) & Volume 4 (NLP),

and other books by **Max Krone** are now available on Amazon.
Just enter **Max Krone** in the **Amazon search bar.**

Disclaimer

The implementation of all information, instructions and strategies contained in this e-book is at your risk. The author cannot assume any liability for any damages of any kind for any legal reason. Liability claims against the author for material or non-material damages caused by the use or non-use of the information or by incorrect and/or incomplete information are excluded theoretically. Any legal and compensation claims are therefore also excluded. This work has been compiled and written down with the utmost care and to the best of our knowledge. However, the author accepts no responsibility for the topicality, completeness and quality of the information. Printing errors and incorrect information cannot be completely excluded. No legal responsibility or liability of any kind can be assumed for incorrect information provided by the author.

Copyright

The content of this book was created and checked with great care. However, no guarantee can be given for the accuracy, completeness and timeliness of the written material, nor for success or failure in the application of what has been read. The content of the book reflects the personal opinion and experience of the author. The content should be interpreted in a way that it serves the purpose of entertainment. It should not be confused with medical assistance. Legal responsibility or liability for counterproductive execution or incorrect interpretation of text and content is not accepted.

Max Krone

Imprint

© Max Krone

2020

All rights reserved.

Reprinting, even in extracts, is not permitted

No part of this work may be reproduced, duplicated or distributed in any form
without written permission of the author.

Represented by:

MAK DIRECT LLC

2880W OAKLAND PARK BLVD, SUITE 225C

OAKLAND PARK, FL 33311

FLORIDA

Made in the USA
Monee, IL
04 June 2020

32552261R00051